MURDER, MARGARET AND ME

by Philip Meeks

SAMUEL FRENCH

samuelfrench.co.uk

Copyright © 2015, 2017 by Philip Meeks
All Rights Reserved

MURDER, MARGARET AND ME is fully protected under the copyright laws of the British Commonwealth, including Canada, the United States of America, and all other countries of the Copyright Union. All rights, including professional and amateur stage productions, recitation, lecturing, public reading, motion picture, radio broadcasting, television and the rights of translation into foreign languages are strictly reserved.

ISBN 978-0-573-11023-8

www.samuelfrench.co.uk

www.samuelfrench.com

For Amateur Production Enquiries

UNITED   KINGDOM   AND   WORLD
EXCLUDING NORTH AMERICA
plays@SamuelFrench-London.co.uk
020 7255 4302/01

Each title is subject to availability from Samuel French,
depending upon country of performance.

CAUTION: Professional and amateur producers are hereby warned that MURDER, MARGARET AND ME is subject to a licensing fee. Publication of this play does not imply availability for performance. Both amateurs and professionals considering a production are strongly advised to apply to the appropriate agent before starting rehearsals, advertising, or booking a theatre. A licensing fee must be paid whether the title is presented for charity or gain and whether or not admission is charged.

The professional rights in this play are controlled by Samuel French Ltd, 24-32 Stephenson Way, London NW1 2HD.

No one shall make any changes in this title for the purpose of production. No part of this book may be reproduced, stored in a retrieval system, or transmitted in any form, by any means, now known or yet to be invented, including mechanical, electronic, photocopying, recording, videotaping, or otherwise, without the prior written permission of the publisher. No one shall upload this title, or part of this title, to any social media websites.

The right of Philip Meeks to be identified as author of this work has been asserted in accordance with Section 77 of the Copyright, Designs and Patents Act 1988.

This text was correct at the time of print and may differ to what is presented on stage.

THINKING ABOUT PERFORMING A SHOW?

There are thousands of plays and musicals available to perform from Samuel French right now, and applying for a licence is easier and more affordable than you might think

From classic plays to brand new musicals, from monologues to epic dramas, there are shows for everyone.

Plays and musicals are protected by copyright law so if you want to perform them, the first thing you'll need is a licence. This simple process helps support the playwright by ensuring they get paid for their work, and means that you'll have the documents you need to stage the show in public.

Not all our shows are available to perform all the time, so it's important to check and apply for a licence before you start rehearsals or commit to doing the show.

LEARN MORE & FIND THOUSANDS OF SHOWS

Browse our full range of plays and musicals and find out more about how to license a show

www.samuelfrench.co.uk/perform

Talk to the friendly experts in our Licensing team for advice on choosing a show, and help with licensing

plays@samuelfrench.co.uk   020 7387 9373

Acting Editions
BORN TO PERFORM

Playscripts designed from the ground up to work the way you do in rehearsal, performance and study

---

Larger, clearer text for easier reading

Wider margins for notes

Performance features such as character and props lists, sound and lighting cues, and more

---

+ CHOOSE A SIZE AND STYLE TO SUIT YOU

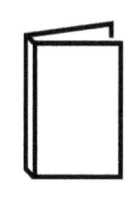

STANDARD EDITION
Our regular paperback book at our regular size

SPIRAL-BOUND EDITION
The same size as the Standard Edition, but with a sturdy, easy-to-fold, easy-to-hold spiral-bound spine

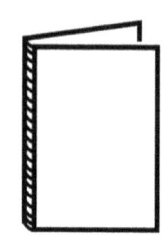

LARGE EDITION
A4 size and spiral bound, with larger text and a blank page for notes opposite every page of text. Perfect for technical and directing use

---

| LEARN MORE | **samuelfrench.co.uk/actingeditions**

Murder, Margaret and Me was first performed at the York Theatre Royal on 17th February 2017.

The cast was as follows:

Margaret Rutherford **Susie Blake**
Agatha Christie **Nichola McAuliffe**
The Spinster **Andrina Carroll**

Written by **Philip Meeks**
Directed by **Damian Cruden**
Designed by **Dawn Allsopp**
Lighting design by **Prema Mehta**
Sound design by **Yvonne Gilbert**

ABOUT THE AUTHOR

Philip's recent work includes *Harpy* which received its World Premiere at Underbelly at the Edinburgh Fringe Festival 2018 and will tour the UK, once again starring Su Pollard, in 2020.

Murder Margaret and Me originally premiered in 2012. It's had productions at York Theatre Royal and Salisbury Playhouse, and also been staged in Mexico and New York, where it won several awards at the New York Festival 2014.

Other plays include *Edith in the Dark*, the first play to be commissioned by Harrogate Theatre in over twenty years. *Kiss me Honey, Honey!* had two sell out seasons in Edinburgh where it won the Fringe First in 2013 and *Clairvoyant* toured the UK with Cath Shipton and Philip Madoc. *Keeping up with the Joan's* starred Susan Penhaligon and was produced by Greenwich Theatre. *Twinkle* about the life of the last Pantomime premiered in 2006 with Tim Healy and went on to have successful productions at York Theatre Royal and the Everyman Cheltenham.

Philip is currently working on several new plays including a family play with music based on Frank L Baum's Oz books.

Philip started his career in television working on *Emmerdale* for five years whilst developing several original series for ITV. He has written regularly for BBC Radio 4, including episodes of their hit legal drama *Brief Lives* and he's developed a string of original ideas for audible. His latest Radio 4 play *Nine Bob Note*s was broadcast in July this year starring Matthew Kelly and is in the process of being adapted for the stage.

AUTHOR'S NOTE

Murder, Margaret and Me started life as a one-person play performed by Janet Prince at the Edinburgh Festival in 2012. It had a sell out run and it returned the following year. It also was a big hit in 2014 at the New York Fringe. I always intending to extend it into a full length play.

The original *Murder, Margaret and Me* focused purely on Margaret Rutherford's story. This new version has allowed me to explore Agatha's too. Due to her famous vanishing trick in 1926 she was also a woman with a secret. As I researched this mysterious incident I began to realise how much Agatha and Margaret had in common, aside from age, physical appearance and their joint status as leading creative forces in a male dominated industry. Their life experiences and personalities seemed to be so entwined, they felt like the same soul. I began to feel quite sad that I'd only imagined their friendship for the purposes of writing the play.

But I was to discover I hadn't entirely made this up after all. The play was performed by Janet two years ago in Torquay as part of the famous Agatha Christie Festival. The place was packed with fans from across the globe, many dressed as Hercule Poirot. At a question and answer session I discussed the fact that I'd made up the details of Agatha and Margaret's friendship. But I was stopped in full flow by one particularly dashing Poirot called Scott Wallace Baker (who has since become a friend) He stood up and declared my assumption was correct.

It transpires the two great women had forged a relationship beyond their awkward meeting on the set of Marple. Scott supplied me with letters from his Christie collection written by Agatha to Stringer Davis after Margaret had fully succumbed to the dementia that would eventually end her life. In these letters Agatha says how much she admired Margaret's portrayal of her spinster. Thankfully I've been able to refer to these letters in this new version of the play. It makes me feel even more that what I've written is as I intended it to be, a play paying homage to the two great women.

Philip Meeks

**Other plays by PHILIP MEEKS
published and licensed by Samuel French**

Edith in the Dark

**FIND PERFECT PLAYS TO PERFORM AT
www.samuelfrench.co.uk/perform**

CHARACTER LIST

GENERAL NOTE

The play's cast of characters features two larger than life famous women. These however, do not need to be portrayed as impersonations. The play works best when they are suggested. Also the age range of the actors can be broad. The characters have a timeless quality so could easily be played by actors in their late forties and above.

AGATHA CHRISTIE – Frustrated by the lack of control she now has over her own work, Agatha turns sleuth to unearth Margaret's past. But will she accept her own in the process? Agatha is sharp, witty and acerbic. She's always been in control. But now she suddenly finds that isn't entirely the case and she has to do something to rectify the situation.

MARGARET RUTHERFORD – A complex character struggling with a terrible secret. She's really two characters. Miss Margaret Rutherford an ebullient comic star celebrated for her eccentric ways. But this eccentricity is cleverly manufactured. Beneath its layers is Peggy whose life was crushed at an early age by fear. She has to make you laugh but then ultimately break your heart.

THE 'SPINSTER' – A delightfully mischievous woman with a wicked glint in her eye. She communicates with the audience as the narrator of the story, manipulates Agatha and Margaret and drives the action by appearing mysteriously in differing guises throughout. She is their inspiration and their conscious. What they draw upon to create their own unique version of the little old lady detective they're both bringing to the screen. She plays the piano in the first few scenes. Obviously the actor playing the role doesn't need to.

NOTE ON STAGING

It states in the text that the actors move their own furniture and props to set the scene. As an alternative, as in the York Theatre Royal and Salisbury Playhouse productions, this can be done by well drilled stage hands or supporting players (who should ideally be middle aged men). As the setting should evoke an abandoned film lot, they should be dressed as set crew.

Due to the nature of her role the Spinster can be involved in the action beyond being a benign presence constantly observing. I haven't included her in many stage directions but she can be at the heart of scenes or to be found on the side-lines with her knitting as desired. I leave this to the invention of the individual directors tackling the play.

PROLOGUE

An empty sound stage. Debris and forgotten old furniture is scattered across the space. This is a place of ghosts, old memories and untold stories.

Downstage right is an area that looks as if it could be a portion of an old set saved from the scrap heap. Comfy chair, cosy lighting and a side table holding a decanter of sherry.

The **SPINSTER** *is discovered here as the audience start to arrive. At first she snoozes gently. At some point she'll awaken and start knitting. She's a fast, furious and determined knitter.*

As the play begins, two figures appear upstage. They take in their surroundings and move slowly centre stepping into the light. **AGATHA CHRISTIE** *and* **MARGARET RUTHERFORD.** *In the story both are kicking seventy. But of course age and looks aren't really important. These performances should offer a suggestion of the people they represent and don't necessarily need to be an exact impersonation.*

They regard each other cautiously. They lock eyes. **MARGARET** *breaks the look first.*

The **SPINSTER** *stops knitting.*

SPINSTER

Oh good. You've both made it.

> **AGATHA** *and* **MARGARET** *turn to the* **SPINSTER**. *They both recognise her.*

I was dreadfully worried my dears. I thought I was going to have to begin without you.

We hear the Miss Marple theme tune from the sixties movies. With the **SPINSTER**'s *help* **AGATHA** *and* **MARGARET** *place the furniture they need for the story they are about to tell.*

ACT ONE

Scene One

MARGARET *and* **AGATHA** *sit apart. They are aware of each other and listen to what each has to say. The* **SPINSTER** *watches them.*

MARGARET *wakes suddenly from a troubling dream. She's vulnerable and anxious. This is not the ebullient Miss Rutherford adored by the public. This is the private side she seldom shows and when she does it's only to those close enough to call her* **PEGGY**.

MARGARET. Where...?

Pause.

India... My dream of India. Near the tamarind tree. The one I was always told to stay away from. It had grown awkwardly but that wouldn't stop the local children from climbing it to steal its fruit. Or me wishing I could. I'd stand in its shade watching them cracking the pods with their teeth and eating the soft bitter flesh, as they chuckled. I wasn't afraid to climb the tree. But I'd never be big enough to reach even the lowest warped branch. I'd never join them.

AGATHA. I rarely sleep for long. Don't dream. Dawn. Best part of the day spent under the Laburnum tree. My killing time. Hypodermics to the jugular. Numerous variations on the fascinating theme of asphyxiation. Multiple stabbings by more than one hand. Slow cooking under the heat of a far eastern sun. A frightful and wonderful array of poisonings. And then there's how to dispatch my murderers. If I feel they deserve it, well off to the gallows with them to swing. If I pity them, as I often do, they'll frequently take their own lives. Then I need to pick their method of suicide. It's exhausting but this is when they are invented. My worst crimes. At this hour. So many endings conjured up at the start of the day.

MARGARET. The smells... they brought my early childhood back to me so vividly. Ripe cardamom. The baked red soil bricks that made up the garden walls, keeping our house safe.

AGATHA. My Archie enjoyed a childhood in India. How romantic.

MARGARET. Rotting meat. A decomposing animal in the process of returning to its maker somewhere close enough for the odour to be carried on the torrid breeze.

AGATHA. We had palm trees in Torquay. That's about as exotic as it got.

MARGARET. The dull clang of a badly made cow bell. A sound that often lulled me to sleep. In this dream it's a warning. And the tree contains no children. And the sun is almost gone and angry... and when I look up... when I look up into the sky dashed with blood. The bruised scarlet of the setting sun...

She snaps back to her senses. Looks around unsure where she is.

Tuft? Tuft?... You're never here when I need you most Tuft. Never... And now I've broken my routine. And when that happens... even the slightest lapse can be problematic.

... It's no good. I can't do it. I simply can't...

I will lose control...

AGATHA. Jolly well join the club. Of course I blame that puffed up and over pomaded oaf for my circumstances. Like I do most things. Poirot. I'd like to remove his ridiculous verbena stiffened moustache. To tell a truth, which nobody knows, it's already happened. He's dead. His last words are concealed in a very deep vault at Coutts. To be published after I've shuffled off, so I don't have to face the music. Well we all have our secrets don't we?

Jane Marple is my diversion. A distraction from the constant demand for the arrogant swine. That's the reason I feel the need to protect her.

They took my name you see. I've only myself to blame. They intend to make "Agatha Christie", what they're calling a brand. Now, I pride myself on being very modern for a Victorian. But vulgarity is so insidious today. Brand! They might as well have gone the whole hog, trussed me up like a side of beef and seared my rear.

Needs must. Unfortunately. I'm used to getting my own way and can bristle, to say the least, when events prevent me. But this is in an altogether different league of tribulation.

They're making my dearest creation... real.

What's to become of Marple?

Scene Two

The **SPINSTER** *chuckles to herself. Finally she addresses the audience.*

SPINSTER I sleep like the dead. Never any qualms. You see, I know I'm an incredible success. Solved my last case only a few weeks ago. Our dear little village piano tuner. He was congenitally deaf, as all the best are. Unfortunately for him this disability, combined with a weakness to the right shin left by a bout of childhood polio, is how his murderer struck with such efficiency. Shocking business. *(She giggles)* I shouldn't laugh. But when I exposed the new village post office boy as the real murderer as well as the victim's illegitimate daughter... that's right, daughter... well my dears. The look on everyone's faces. The postmistress still won't serve me on pension day. Moments such as that help me sleep at night. Lost in a land of such delightful dreams.

She takes up her knitting.

You'll excuse me if I carry on? I find I need to keep the flow going when the yarn is freshly cast. And you'll forgive me if I don't introduce myself? I seldom do. Ignore me if the fancy takes you. Pretend I'm not here. Though I'd suggest it would be wise to pay close attention.

You all know me by the way, so strictly speaking introductions aren't a necessity. You've grown up with me. On the page. In your heads. You all have a mind's eye image of me I'm sure. Well, my dears, here I am in the flesh, full blooded and real. How exciting for you.

You'll have also, in all probability, caught me in the corner of your living rooms. In various forms, shapes and sizes. Some I'd rather forget. Some particularly celebrated... Of course that's why we're here.

The entertainment you are about to see is part enchantment and part investigation! There's been every effort made to wrap it up snugly in a fairytale of sorts but at its centre there's a puzzle to solve. A pattern to be unpicked stitch by stitch. It'll be thrilling. Trust me. I'm a little old lady.

Pause.

The incredible women you've already met were both celebrated at the start of their acquaintance, at an age when they should have been winding down. Staying at home knitting! One can only imagine what the fairer sex will go on to achieve in your time my dears. Although I feel life was far simpler when we knew our place. And remained there.

An earthy chuckle. Like she ever did that.

As dear as Agatha is to my heart I'd like you to pay particular attention to the other lady. Miss Margaret Rutherford. Peggy to her friends. There's far more to her than meets the eye. Of course you can say that about almost anyone. Just glancing out at you all now... well lies are seldom very well disguised. Even if you've lived with them a lifetime.

Oh, and I've foolishly neglected to point out one crucial fact, my dears.

The only real truth in our story is that Rutherford, the Funniest Woman Alive, didn't want anybody to know the truth.

Scene Three

MARGARET *has now adopted the persona we all know her for. She's poised by a phone. Christmas bells ring out.*

MARGARET. "I have survived the birth of the airplane, the death of the corset, short hair and two world wars".

These aren't my own words alas. They belong to a cherished character I once played. But to them I would personally contribute, the advent of "the jive", a plethora of "falsies", paper underwear, instant bread sauce. And of course... the tax man.

AGATHA *is on the phone. She's irritated.*

AGATHA. Tell him I'll hold.

MARGARET. It's with a heavy heart that I've reached my decision.

MARGARET *starts to dial.*

AGATHA. That's right... Mrs Christie... and I'm not going anywhere until I speak with him.

Honestly. Daphne got Hitchcock. I get Pollock.

I ploughed through their God awful script and told them emphatically that she can't be in every scene. She doesn't function like that. Mr Pollock won't be dissuaded. He's promised me a star. I've tried to explain one simple fact. Miss Marple isn't a star. She's... mine.

MARGARET. Good day to you Mr Pollock... That's correct, it is she...

AGATHA. No... unexpected or not I can't afford to wait for him to return my call. Not again. You see I'm really not getting any younger... thank you.

MARGARET. Mr Stringer Davis and myself wish you the very merriest of Christmas's. Merry Christmas to you all.

AGATHA. It's enough to make one resort to a fit of blasphemous rage.

MARGARET. Yes the bells are quite delightful aren't they? It's actually the mid-morning service from Winchester on the wireless.

AGATHA. But I'm determined to keep a firm grip on my dignity.

MARGARET. It's a festive tradition here at Nine Elms to have the wireless turned up full blast while Stringer grapples with the goose. And today it is setting a momentous tone for what I'm about to tell you.

AGATHA. Hello George. We speak again at last. If I were prone to paranoia I'd be more than a tiny bit concerned that you were trying to avoid me. I gather you have some news.

MARGARET. And may I say before I make my announcement, this is the very best Christmas present you're ever likely to receive...

Miss Margaret Rutherford will be playing your Miss Jane Marple.

AGATHA. Christ...

Scene Four

The **SPINSTER** *has returned to her knitting.*

SPINSTER. I'm unsure what this is going to be as yet, but when you've spent as long as I have following patterns you understand the way the wool will twist and turn and take on form. It becomes an instinct. This ability can also be applied to other matters. If you're astute, you should be able to spot when something in human nature is going awry. Hopefully before everything unravels.

To make my point let me begin a tale of two gentlemen. And this is important so listen. Imagine them. A dignified clergyman with his son, on holiday together in the country to take long relaxing walks. But are these walks truly relaxing? The son is pacing ahead a few steps stifling tears. The father follows persistently. Talking. His tone tinged with desperation. The pattern doesn't fit. Their behaviour is off kilter to say the very least.

Pause.

Remember these chaps. We will return to them in due course.

Margaret and Agatha first meet at a momentous occasion. The launch of the most anticipated picture for some time… I miss the silent days of course. That's how I honed my musical flair. Oh yes. I can tickle the ivories. There's so much about me that would surprise you my dears. So much! I accompanied many a screening at the village hall before the war. All the vicars insisted… and we got through a lot of those. But listen to me. Terrible habit. Turning the story back to oneself.

Lights change.

Scene Five

> **MARGARET** *and* **AGATHA** *face each other smile politely, hide each other's anxiety. Shake hands awkwardly.*

MARGARET. Thrilling yes... a new adventure. Always thrilling. And an honour? Well...

AGATHA. Delighted.

MARGARET. Absolutely delighted.

AGATHA. Thrilled.

> *Silence. Another question is posed.*

MARGARET. Oh certainly. All these years. My marvellous career. It's passed like a dream. So much so I can't quite believe we've reached the sixties. I will take everything this decade brings in my stride.

AGATHA. I echo that sentiment.

MARGARET. Even this film.

> **AGATHA** *throws* **MARGARET** *a look.*

I mean... well... the first day in front of the camera will swiftly be upon us. Always unnerving. The start of another escapade. On this occasion, an excursion into dark territory. For me at least. However it may be gussied up; murder is not something to be taken lightly.

> *A pause. Another question asked.*

AGATHA. No questions about the Belgian! Today is about my spinster. I created her with my grandmother in mind. Diminutive. Bird like.

> *She looks to* **MARGARET** *for a beat.*

Peppermints and a powdered smile masking her true intent. Experienced in human nature and skilled in telling you about it. Often without saying a word. She knew you didn't need to be nice to be good. A sweet little old lady on the outside. As sweet as strychnine within. I loved my grandmother.

> *Another question.*

MARGARET. Yes indeed. That's correct. I did turn down the role. Several times. Tuft persuaded me in the end. "See it like a game of chess" he said "one she's playing for the greater good."

Sorry? Tuft... that's the special name I have for my dear husband, that very fine actor Mr Stringer Davis. He'll be joining me in the picture. My sidekick of sorts.

AGATHA. She doesn't have a side kick...

MARGARET. You see a little quif of his hair always misbehaved. Whenever I saw him, there would be Tuft. Stubbornly erect. This was when we first met of course. During our courtship. The early years. Fifteen or so of the happiest I've ever known. I must add that his follicles are far more subdued these days. What's left of them. However it was a very endearing little quirk of nature while it lasted. My Tuft.

AGATHA. That's delightful Miss Rutherford. But why did you turn the part down? I for one am fascinated.

Awkward beat. **MARGARET** *isn't sure what she says. But she decides to be honest and offer the truth as she sees it.*

MARGARET. Because I have a reputation to maintain, Mrs Christie. Fans who have remained loyal for many years. I owe them. I don't wish to be connected to anything that I deem to be sordid.

AGATHA. Sordid!

MARGARET. But I'll find a way to play her. Make the proceedings more palatable.

AGATHA. Oh you will, will you...

MARGARET. I'll do her proud. And you Mrs Christie.

I will tackle whatever evil gets thrown my way with gusto. I will be every inch the outwardly genteel but inwardly seething lady amateur sleuth. I will play this character with all my heart. And they may have wanted Margaret Rutherford. She's the funniest woman alive they say. Well I'm afraid, and I'm certain Miss Marple would agree with me on this, I have never found murder amusing.

Scene Six

AGATHA *is banging away at her typewriter. The* **SPINSTER** *joins her.*

AGATHA. I'm not going to let her get away with that.

SPINSTER. Marple relishes murder. It's why she exists.

AGATHA. Exactly.

SPINSTER. Had there not been so many murders to keep her busy in St. Mary Mead, she'd have probably committed a few herself.

AGATHA. The glint in her eye? Solid steel. And Miss Marple never applied herself with "gusto".

SPINSTER. Dear me, no. Leave the all guns blazing approach to those brash Americans, Mr Spade and Mr Marlowe. The spinster will always be found on the sidelines where she belongs...

AGATHA. Forgive me if my vexation is unsettling.

SPINSTER. Don't worry dear.

AGATHA. I'm not used to having the opportunity to speak my mind.

SPINSTER. Carry on. Let it all out.

AGATHA. My feelings are usually only given vent to, second hand. When some imagined victim or other is getting their brains smashed in.

SPINSTER. One of your favourites.

AGATHA. Certainly top ten. As a rule I tend to like my victims far less than my murderers. That's the nature of evil. And my method of constructing a path through evil has never failed me. A solid formula.

SPINSTER. I'm sure that's exactly how Miss Rutherford approaches her performances...

AGATHA. I very much doubt there's anything resembling finesse...

SPINSTER. You were a bit mean. Don't you think?

AGATHA. What? She started it.

SPINSTER. I'm merely making an observation.

AGATHA. Well I'd rather you didn't old woman.

SPINSTER. The bird like remark was still uncalled for.

AGATHA. I had a valid point to make. Bird like's one thing Rutherford's clearly not. Unless the bird in question lived a few million years ago, with the wing span of a Boeing 707. It could have been worse. I could have quoted some of her notices. "It's true Miss Rutherford. You do have a face like a poached egg."

SPINSTER. You can't stand not being in control.

AGATHA. Can you blame me? In my books I make all the choices. Now it seems I have to let them go. Agatha Christie is Limited. At least they chose the right word. Limited.

Pause.

SPINSTER. Doesn't something fascinate you about Miss Rutherford?

AGATHA. Why should I be interested in her?

SPINSTER. Her sadness?

AGATHA. That was fear. Many people feel intimidated by me.

SPINSTER. It was far more than that.

AGATHA. I'm going to stop talking to you now. Something indescribably horrific is about to be discovered in the outhouse.

AGATHA *types away. The* SPINSTER *knits.*

SPINSTER. Let's return to our two gentlemen for a moment. They had reserved a twin room at a little bed and breakfast for one week. The landlady would say later, her dealings with the pair gave no indication of the devastation that ultimately came to pass.

AGATHA. What are you wittering on about now?

SPINSTER. I'm musing. Wondering why you seem so determined to let a story slip between your fingers. Because there's a good one behind Miss Rutherford bluster. There has to be.

AGATHA. No good. Can't concentrate.

SPINSTER. There must be a way you can grab back some control? Turn things to your advantage.

AGATHA. You're right. Must be.

Pause.

SPINSTER. Pay a visit? Go and see them do a spot of filming?

AGATHA. Unannounced. Uninvited. What a good idea. I'll give Miss Margaret Rutherford sordid.

SPINSTER. What better way to get to understand her. Catch her unawares.

AGATHA. Grandmother always knows best.

Scene Seven

AGATHA. Did it. Visited the set unannounced and frightfully early. There before she was. Didn't have to wait long. My first sight of her was as she arrived. On a pony and trap.

Sound of pony and trap.

MARGARET. One of the more agreeable points about taking on this role was it offered me freedom.

AGATHA. Seriously?

MARGARET. It was so close to home I could travel to the set, in any way I wished.

AGATHA. She trundled into Elstree Studios quite majestically. What was that all about?

MARGARET. Making an entrance. Miss Margaret Rutherford always knows how to set the right tone.

AGATHA. She held her head aloft, like a cloud. White and woolly with undulating features you needed to pick out with care. Quite a display.

MARGARET. I caught her eye quite by chance. Damn and blast! I thought the publicity call would have been the last I'd see of her... the producers had said as much but there she was. I looked away quickly. Pretended I hadn't seen her.

AGATHA. Though I knew she had. Oh yes. And I'd unsettled her. Muddled up in that eccentric barrage was something bewildered. Slightly lost.

MARGARET. I forgot myself. Gently lashed Fudge the pony three times instead of two and she set off in a canter heading for the back lot.

AGATHA. Chippies scattered cursing. A make-up girl screamed in a flurry of multi-coloured curlers. She almost lost control of her horse!

MARGARET. Almost! I never lose control. I can't afford to. Not completely.

I looked back. Unintentionally caught Mrs Christie's eye again. Fiddlesticks! Oh behave yourself Fudge!

AGATHA CHRISTIE. And in that instant I sensed intrigue. I can never resist intrigue.

Theme music.

Scene Eight

The theme tune plays.

MARGARET. They said of me once:

"Only one woman can dress so nonchalantly and get away with it. Only one woman can knot a scarf so jauntily, button a cardigan so carelessly, and clasp a handbag so ineffectively. When the total result is Margaret Rutherford all we can do is cheer."

One of the ways I feel sure I can master Marple is by supplying my own attire. I like to bring my particular style to as many roles I can, especially those set in the modern day. You have to watch these costume designers and their fancy ideas. When one's bosoms have achieved a certain girth, you can't afford to be reckless with the way they're presented.

She puts on the cape and scarf and strikes a pose. She becomes the Miss Marple so many remember!

I will also insist on doing my own stunts. The audience wants Miss Margaret Rutherford and I feel it's my duty to supply an ample portion of her at least. It won't be quiet what they're expecting from me. But how rip-roaring will that be for them?

The scripts call for regular scrapes. I'll clamber up railway embankments, give chase, ride side saddle, fence and vigorously pull off Robert Morley's riding boots. In one especially daring sequence I will even attempt… the twist. Quite an engaging dance when performed by the younger generation. My take on it will probably make me look like I am trying to pop a recalcitrant hip back into its wayward socket.

Pause.

It's been quite a day. Quite a day.

My first line on screen as Miss Marple is, "A woman has been strangled. I saw it." Strangled. I delivered it with such anguish. I could tell they were taken aback. No half look to the camera with a wobble of the jowls. No. It's important I respect this material. It's the only way…

Poor Pearl, make-up lady. The incident with Fudge distressed her terribly. She laddered her new stockings so I dispatched

Tuft at once to replace them and replenish the kirby grips lost in the fray.

The **SPINSTER** *takes on the guise of Pearl.*

SPINSTER. You sure Miss Rutherford?

MARGARET. I insist.

SPINSTER. Only they come out my wages you see.

MARGARET. We certainly can't have that.

Pause.

SPINSTER. It was her. Wasn't it? Today. Mrs Christie?

MARGARET. I believe so.

SPINSTER. Everyone was saying. Her spectacles kept catching the lights at the back of the studio.

MARGARET. Most distracting.

SPINSTER. She stood so still. No expressions. Spoke to no one. Gave nothing away.

MARGARET. Why would she be here to give anything "away"?

SPINSTER. Wish I'd known she were coming.

MARGARET. Nobody knew. Didn't you see Mr Pollock collide with camera two when she loomed up large in front of him?

SPINSTER. I'd have brought something for her to sign. Her murders are the best. I can't get enough of crime books, me.

MARGARET. We can't all be perfect.

SPINSTER. And like I said on day one as I crimped your hair, I especially love the Marple's. Read the lot. As I'm sure you have.

Beat. **MARGARET** *laughs.*

Miss Marple puts me in mind of Myrtle Firbank who ran our corner shop way back when. Always has. Not in the same class mind you. Not by half. Old Myrtle had a fondness for spitting her lungs up on the shop floor. But there wasn't another grocers nearby so everyone put up with it. And watched where they stepped.

MARGARET. I can always rely on you Pearl, for the most appealing of images.

SPINSTER. But Myrtle was wily. Cunning as they come. No one pilfered as much as an inch of licorice root, 'cause they'd be found out. Every time. She'd round up us nippers, all five-foot-nothing of her, and tell us what she knew and how she knew it. Then there'd be holy hell to pay.

MARGARET. Am I doing her justice?

SPINSTER. Who?

MARGARET. Miss Marple.

SPINSTER. What you asking me for?

MARGARET. You're obviously an aficionado.

SPINSTER. If you say so... whatever one of them is when they're at home.

Silence.

MARGARET. I heard the rumours. That girl who serves the morning tea.

SPINSTER. Pay no attention to her. Gormless gossip. And she can't make a decent brew.

MARGARET. I had noticed.

SPINSTER. Hasn't the sense she was born with, that one.

MARGARET. You don't need to protect me. I took my concerns to Mr. Pollock himself. His face answered my question. He tried to placate me. Mumbled something about Mrs Christie having concerns in general about her stories being filmed. It didn't wash.

SPINSTER. I wouldn't give it another thought.

MARGARET. I can't understand it. As I said to one of the other actresses only yesterday, I would appreciate Mrs Christie's concerns if we were working in *(mock horror)* the television. But we are creating a motion picture. This is the silver screen. One's inventions being immortalised in such a way... well... it has to be magnificent. I said "Imagine Miss Marple on the television, and shudder." She agreed obviously. Lovely girl. Hasn't had much of a career, dear Joan Hickson.

SPINSTER. Bless her.

MARGARET. Mrs Christie doesn't like the script.

SPINSTER. Writers. Funny lot.

MARGARET. Doesn't like the fact that I'm donning various guises throughout the picture.

SPINSTER. Miss Marple's always popping up where you least expect her. Acting as a confidante. Helping to move the plot along. That's her way.

Pause.

MARGARET. You avoided my question Pearl.

SPINSTER. Really? I'm certain I didn't.

MARGARET. Am I doing her justice?

SPINSTER. Course you are. I've always been a fan of yours. Daresay you'd never make a bad job of any part…

MARGARET. So I'm an engaging Marple simply by virtue of the fact that I'm Miss Margaret Rutherford…?

SPINSTER. No. That's not what I meant. Now stop it. Honestly you ladies and your insecurities. You're almost as bad as Anna Neagle when she learned she was being filmed in Technicolor. Had to coax her out of the ladies powder room with half a packet of Huntley and Palmers ginger nuts.

Pause.

MARGARET. Tell me more about this old woman Miss Marple reminds you of…

SPINSTER. Not much more to say. Except I reckon that's why we all love reading about Miss Marple. She reminds us all of someone we've known.

MARGARET. My Aunt Bessie. She could be an odd one

SPINSTER. That's how she gets under your skin.

MARGARET ponders this.

MARGARET. Fancied herself a psychic. She was quite sure that if one asked a dead relative to intercede personally with God for something sensible like a new pair of Sunday shoes there was a good chance the prayer would be granted.

Pearl finishes with MARGARET's hair.

SPINSTER. There. All done. *(Pause)* Why not take her to tea?

MARGARET. Mrs Christie? I'm sure our producers…

SPINSTER. You two might as well be in charge around here. Should see the way the big-wigs flap at the mention of your names. Getting to know each other might sort out your silly worries.

The SPINSTER leaves MARGARET but watches her.

MARGARET. Tuft could fetch the Rockingham. Or we could invite her to Nine Elms to meet the family. She'll adore the family. That's a decision made. You don't need the mind of a Marple to know when the air is in need of a little genteel clearing.

Music. The **SPINSTER** *is herself again and she's cracking on with her knitting.*

SPINSTER. There. It didn't take too much of my cunning to nudge them together.

I do hope, by the way, you haven't forgotten our pair of elegant gentlemen taking a break from it all? Replenishing their resources by immersing themselves in the country air?

Soon we will return to them. And I'm afraid it won't be pretty.

All I'll reveal for now is… they were perfect guests. Dependable, quiet, respectful and always on time, to second, for the meals included in their bed and board. Their landlady, a Mrs Marchant, took particular delight that both men were tee-total.

She takes up a very full glass of sherry.

Chin, chin!

She takes a healthy gulp.

Scene Nine

We're at Nine Elms. MARGARET *is anxious preparing Afternoon Tea.* AGATHA *arrives with a large carpet bag. The* SPINSTER *hovering nearby.* MARGARET *ushers* AGATHA *in. The pair are being incredibly polite.*

MARGARET. Mrs Christie.....Welcome...

AGATHA. What a delightful room.

MARGARET. Welcome to our little nest.

AGATHA. And so much... stuff.

MARGARET. Yes. Everything we love. We pride ourselves on being home-makers Tuft and I. And we take great delight in our home feeling as much of a home to our guests. And the family of course. And dear friends who deserve the very best because they remind me who I am... so make yourself comfortable Mrs Christie. Make yourself at home. Please.

AGATHA. Will Mr Davis be joining us?

MARGARET. No, no. Stringer is on a mission. Off to Fortnum's for fresh supplies. I've always insisted on spending whatever is required, on necessities to oil the wheels. Where would we be without luxury?

AGATHA. Where indeed.

Pause.

MARGARET. Ginger marmalade for example.

AGATHA. *(Surprised)* Really?

MARGARET. Can't live without it. Chocolate for a midnight feast. Tea brewed in fine china. bottles. Egg cosies. You can't have a tepid boiled egg; it would disappoint the soldiers. I won't go anywhere without my luxuries. Often when we travel Stringer follows behind, weighed down like my very own private Sherpa.

AGATHA. I myself depend on Fortnum's excellent delivery service.

MARGARET. Tuft doesn't really get out much aside from the odd invigorating country walk. He's very fond of nature. He'll make a day of it today. Take in a matinee. Probably catch Constance Shacklock in the *Sound of Music*. Again. He loves her. After the show he'll have a rarebit at The Criterion. Then, without a shadow of a doubt, he'll get up to mischief of one sort or another with our dear friend Johnny Gielgud. Do you know Mr Gielgud's work?

AGATHA. I believe I once saw half of his Hamlet.

MARGARET. He and Stringer are very close. Men need their own from time to time. Don't you agree? Boys will be boys. Now a toast. I'd offer you a nip of brandy or....

AGATHA. *(In)* I don't indulge.

MARGARET. Just as well. Tuft always locks the tantalus and takes the tiny key with him when he goes out. Force of habit. His mother you see. Dipsomania can be most distressing. Probably why she lived so very long. Fortified. Well, we will toast our new acquaintance with tea.

She laughs and goes to sort out tea. AGATHA *directs her speech to the* SPINSTER.

AGATHA. That laugh was forced. As was the agitated display of talking up this stiflingly cluttered room. Honestly. If only actors wouldn't act! Miss Margaret Rutherford is the greatest role of her career.

MARGARET *brings tea on a trolley...*

MARGARET. Here we are. Afternoon tea. Best meal of the day.

AGATHA. I was just admiring your well stocked book shelves.

MARGARET. Something for everyone's tastes. We're big readers. Nothing like it on a cosy night is there. Roaring fire. Crumpets and the trusty toasting fork at hand in case one gets peckish. A blanket over your knees and an engrossing tome. Bliss.

AGATHA. Interesting. Toasting fork.

AGATHA *makes a note in a tiny black book.* MARGARET *watches.*

MARGARET. Sorry. After so very many best sellers one is constantly on the lookout for new murder weapons. Can't seem to spot any of my titles up there.

MARGARET. Really? I trust you like your tea to be brewed sturdily.

AGATHA. I can pick out my name a mile away. None there.

MARGARET. And I always add two for the pot.

AGATHA. You are familiar with my novels?

MARGARET. Who isn't? You're the Queen of Crime.

AGATHA. So you've read me?

MARGARET. Of course… not.

I mean…

afternoon tea isn't afternoon tea without delicious cake.

Awkward laugh she produces a cake and starts slicing it vigorously.

AGATHA. So you haven't read anything. Not even a Poirot?

MARGARET. I hear he's a sheer delight.

AGATHA. Anything but. Find out for yourself.

She produces two books from the carpet bag. Hands them to MARGARET.

Not firsts but I've signed them.

MARGARET. I tend to favour non-fiction. History?

AGATHA *produces another book.*

AGATHA. Ancient Egypt? *Death Comes As The End.* Bit of a buzz about this one. I created an entire sub-genre. The historical who-dunnit.

MARGARET. Jean Plaidy always captures a period, don't you think?

AGATHA. The horrors in history are far more gruesome than my inventions. As a rule I never dispatch more than three people per novel…

MARGARET. Or romance. Who can resist romance? I'm always touched by the Bronte's. *Wuthering Heights…*

AGATHA. In which everybody dies… so this might *pique* your interest.

Produces another book. MARGARET *scans the title…*

MARGARET. 'And Then There Were None'.

AGATHA. As the title suggests; not many left to turn off the lights at the end.

MARGARET. And there's so many modern authors who have a flair for affairs of the heart… I hear Mary Westmacott's works are wonderful.

AGATHA. They most certainly are.

MARGARET. You're a fan?

AGATHA. I am Mary Westmacott!!

She produces two more tomes triumphantly.

AGATHA. The one on top? Written in less than a week.

MARGARET. Really?

AGATHA. Given up on romance these days.

MARGARET. What a pity.

Pause.

AGATHA. So which do you fancy delving into first?

MARGARET. More cake! *(to herself)* She'll shut up after more cake.

She manically slices the cake. Something whizzes past AGATHA *as* MARGARET *mangles the cake.*

MARGARET. Sorry. A wayward walnut.

Beat. AGATHA *fishes a walnut out of her cup of tea.*

AGATHA. I'd hate to get on the wrong end of that cake slice.

MARGARET *struggles to find a diversion. She's suddenly inspired.*

MARGARET. How would you like to meet the family?

AGATHA. Are they joining us?

MARGARET. They seldom miss afternoon tea.

AGATHA. Where are they?

MARGARET. Well you're sitting on one of them.

MARGARET *rummages for a bit, then finds a stuffed bunny behind* AGATHA.

This is Minnie who's been with us… I can't recall since when. But forever. Say hello to Agatha, Minnie. *(As Minnie)* "Hello Mrs Christie".

AGATHA. *(Stunned)* How… charming… what a lovely little stuffed… mouse?

MARGARET. Rabbit dear. And talk directly to her. She doesn't like to be patronised.

AGATHA. Terribly sorry…

MARGARET. She's a very practical bunny. If Tuft and I have one of our very rare domestic skirmishes, Minnie tells him quite plainly that she's feeling huffy today. Works every time. Off he goes on one of his walks. Nature calling him hither.

She places the toy on the table.

I think she's fond of you.

AGATHA. How…. delightful…

MARGARET *produces another toy. A cat.*

MARGARET. And this is Nicodemus and he's of royal origin given to us by none other than his gracious highness Prince Juan of Jordan. "A pleasure to meet you Mrs Christie".

AGATHA. Please. Call me Agatha... I mean...

AGATHA *catches herself.*

MARGARET. And then there's the others. They all have their own unique place in my heart.

AGATHA. Margaret...

MARGARET. Peggy dear. Call me Peggy. Please. We know each other well enough now.

AGATHA. We don't. But I'd like to...

MARGARET. Then I'll gather the rest of the family. They all have stories of their own to tell.

AGATHA. But I want to know your story.

Pause.

MARGARET. No. That wouldn't be right. It is my job to tell your story. I will bring Miss Marple to life with sincerity and integrity. You have my assurance. I tell you this because... well... you see... I know you weren't keen... on me. Playing her...

Pause.

Noise off. Someone fumbling with a lock.

MARGARET. Stringer. He shouldn't be back this early.

AGATHA. (*To the Spinster*) And Peggy had gone. Like a light switch. Margaret Rutherford was back in charge.

MARGARET. His outing has been curtailed by mischief. Wait until I see Johnny Gielgud. Played one of his stupid tricks. Slipped out of the tiny lift at Fortnum's giggling like a school girl whilst jamming the cage door behind him. It took two hours to free Tuft! Meanwhile Johnny was having a ball in Soho. And Tuft is so fond of his Soho sojourns... he assures me there's some top-notch coffee shops.

AGATHA. Teatime was over.

Scene Ten

AGATHA *joins the* SPINSTER.

AGATHA. I'd threatened her in some way and as a reaction she'd transformed into a child sharing her world... a child.

SPINSTER. A family of stuffed toys?

AGATHA. Yes.

SPINSTER. And to think our second to last vicar's wife almost got committed for talking to her cat. Looking back, how I wish I hadn't intervened and saved her. Then she mightn't have been poisoned at the alter. A homicidal flower arranger, peeved at being relieved of her duties decorating the vestry.

AGATHA. Is that everything?

SPINSTER. Cause of death, belladonna.

AGATHA. In the communion wine?

SPINSTER. Atropine causes such an excruciating departure.

AGATHA *notes this down quickly completing a section of a story whilst laughing to herself.*

AGATHA. This one's going to put the wind up the Women's Institute. How wonderful.

SPINSTER. But on the whole tea at Nine Elms was a triumph?

AGATHA. Yes. Until the husband arrived. He of the bland persona and inane grin. I'm really not fond of him.

At least it's confirmed that there's more behind her reluctance to play Miss Marple than believing it to be beneath her. Something had happened to her. Something way back that haunted her still. Secrets. They can be deadly.

SPINSTER. You're a fine one to talk.

AGATHA. If not dealt with they can lead to disaster. I have experience of secrets.

SPINSTER. Why don't you tell them? I dare you.

Pause.

AGATHA. Do you think I should?

SPINSTER. Since most of them are only really interested in Margaret at this point, it might add a bit of colour to your character.

AGATHA. But as a writer I'm used to my audience appreciating me in a different way. An author isn't needy. Isn't yearning for constant love and admiration. But if you all insist. Here it is. My secret. The truth.

Of the thirty six ways of avoiding disaster, running away is the best. Chinese proverbs. One for every occasion.

Although I didn't run away. I really didn't.

SPINSTER. Agatha...

AGATHA. Eleven days. That was all. Such a fuss. I vanished you see. So completely and effectively, it became a matter of national concern. A mystery that even outwitted Sherlock Holmes. Or the next best thing. Arthur Conan Doyle used one of my gloves to hold a séance. He engaged the finest clairvoyants in Europe in his attempts to make contact with me on the other side. I wrote to him when I'd returned and thanked him for his valiant efforts. He didn't write back.

The 3rd of December 1926. A cold Friday evening when the days were at their shortest. I often ate alone at Styles, my gloomy home. Archie my beloved was so very often away or terribly late. Max Mallowan is my second husband. Married him and got a title thrown in for good measure. He's as solid as a mahogany sideboard. Or one of the slabs of fossil raddled granite he takes such delight in chipping away at.

The world will never remember Archibald Christie. I took his name as fame descended. That's when things started going wrong. I truly believe he hated me for it. But I kept it. Made it my own. That was part of my revenge.

What I put him through until I was discovered... I don't regret it. If I had, would I have been found doing a vigorous solo Charleston at a well-heeled Christmas Ball in Harrogate's finest hotel...?

I claimed not to remember anything. Truth is I couldn't tell a soul.

Pause. We see **AGATHA***'s pain as she remembers. She decides against telling the truth.*

I was undercover. It was the Bolsheviks. Poisoning the very fabric of our genteel society. Brainwashing our children through insidious means. A travelling circus. No one suspected that under the Big Top hid a highly organised cell of Mother Russia's warped political hooligans headed by a twenty-two-stone bearded lady. She was said to be Rasputin's Godmother.

SPINSTER. Stop now...

AGATHA. So I joined the circus.

SPINSTER. We're no longer listening.

AGATHA. As a lady lion tamer!

SPINSTER. Agatha! You make things up.

> **AGATHA** *looks at the* **SPINSTER** *incredulously.*

AGATHA. Well don't ask me again old woman. My secret stays here. In my heart. Where it's not harming me.

SPINSTER. Of course it's not.

AGATHA. Although I really feel the same can't be said for my new acquaintance...

Scene Eleven

AGATHA *and* **MARGARET** *are alone again at Nine Elms. This time they're having dinner.*

AGATHA. Perhaps he could spontaneously combust!

Ideally I'd like him to be taken as spectacularly as possible whilst he's carried away and in full flow. Those tiresome little grey cells ring o each other as he talks about himself in the third person and tells everyone, yet again, who killed who, where and why. Perhaps he could miss his step. Fall over a balustrade mid-sentence or topple awkwardly down half a dozen marble steps. Or he could fail to realise that since he's taken so long to get to the point the killer is now behind him with a cosh.

MARGARET. Or you could merely stop writing about your Mr Poirot.

AGATHA. They'd never allow it. Never. My readers. I've only got myself to blame. Everywhere I go people want to know about him. Not me. Not really. I don't mind as such.

MARGARET. I used to like to ride my bike. Without fail as I sailed by, people would shout out "There she goes… There's Arcati" I don't know why. I've done lots of lovely pictures. And lovely plays. I've had a wonderful career.

AGATHA. Success. It never really goes the way one wants it.

Pause.

MARGARET. I've been mulling something over. All those words… How do you do it?

AGATHA. I didn't think you cared.

MARGARET. I'm interested.

AGATHA. Well… You think of the story.

MARGARET. Yes…

AGATHA. Then you sit down and write it.

MARGARET. There has to be more to it than that.

AGATHA. Not much.

MARGARET. That's like me saying I learn the lines and trundle on set.

AGATHA. Well what else do you do?

MARGARET. Observe. Never stop. Stashing people away like mementos. Slight slivers of them they'll never miss or notice. A sigh. A frown. And most importantly glances.

MARGARET *gives examples of three glances. Pause.*

AGATHA. They all looked exactly the same.

MARGARET. Well they weren't. Not to me at least and as far as the audience is concerned that's what matters.

You must always be observing. Searching for new ideas. New stories.

Awkward laugh from AGATHA.

AGATHA. Oh no... I have plenty of those stored up and stashed away. Plenty.

She changes the subject.

How's the reading going?

MARGARET. Ah yes... Well... I've had so many lines to cram in... it never gets any easier...

AGATHA. I can't see the novels I gave you.

MARGARET. They're here somewhere. I saw Tuft thumbing Mrs McGinty only the other day...

AGATHA. How's Stringer faring?

MARGARET. His weak chest is such a hindrance to him. He's tucked up with *The Times*. I'll pop in with a poultice later.

AGATHA. Thank him for a lovely meal.

MARGARET. It was nothing. The pie was from our local butchers. We can't get enough of them.

AGATHA. And the sauce?

MARGARET. Campbell's Condensed Cream of Tomato. And the knack is to warm it through but keep it condensed. That way it's much richer.

AGATHA. Not to mention unusual.

MARGARET. He'll be back on set soon I'm certain. A professional. And isn't he good in the role of Mr Stringer.

AGATHA. Stringer's playing...

MARGARET. Mr Stringer. Yes.

AGATHA. I'd forgotten that.

MARGARET. And he thought of the character name all by himself. He's a very perceptive actor. Touched. With a precious gift.

AGATHA. Touched… yes.

Pause.

MARGARET. I suspect now of course, as well as Madam Arcati, I'll also be known as Miss Marple. We'll be joined. You and I. In the public consciousness.

Pause.

AGATHA. Why did you finally agree to play her Peggy?

Pause.

MARGARET. Like I told you. My weakness for life's little luxuries. Necessities always tend to seem less important. I'm happy to admit this is a tad foolish. It has led to unopened letters crammed in drawers, telephone calls not returned and on one occasion a crushing case of lumbago. I'm really too old to crouch behind sofas with Tuft, however much fun it might be. However desperate we are to avoid the taxman at the door.

AGATHA. Ah. The taxman. Him.

MARGARET. You too? Oh dear. Well we found ourselves in a shocking state of affairs. I've even had to appear on the television. *(Mock horror)* The television! We nearly lost the house.

AGATHA. I lost my name. It's practically taking a life on of its own. Most disconcerting.

MARGARET. It seemed a certainty that we would have to sell it. I couldn't allow that to happen. I didn't care much for the suggestions others offered. They were in way of support but the very idea of losing our home. Coward wrote. "Come to Jamaica. The weather's perfect for old bones. Stringer will find some of the locals invigorating."

But Tuft is loyal.

Pause.

AGATHA. Why didn't you want to play her Peggy?

    MARGARET *becomes vulnerable. A clock chimes. A diversion.*

MARGARET. Time for pudding. Blancmange in our little bunny mold. But we have to make a huge decision. Who's going to have Mrs Bunny's head and who's going to have, my favourite, her little tail. Although we'll have to make sure none of the family hear us when we're dividing her up. They get quite twitchy.

MARGARET *goes.* AGATHA *turns to the* SPINSTER.

AGATHA. Alone at last. I seized the chance to look for clues in the living room. Where is Peggy? Nothing there. All fake. All show. The inner sanctum at the heart of her home. All part of the routine. She'd perfected the construction of Miss Margaret Rutherford right down to the very last stuffed toy.

MARGARET *now has a torch. The lights dim as she explores.*

I ventured out into the rest of the house. The hallway was cold. A draught blew in from an unused chimney close to the kitchen. I heard movement above. Climbed the stairs. If caught...

SPINSTER. Well, even a world famous author needs to spend a penny.

AGATHA. Precisely... a loose floorboard groaned and echoed so I dipped into the first room I passed. I was startled at what I found.

SPINSTER. Go on... I'm gripped.

AGATHA. A bare cold space. Such a contrast to the living room. Sterile. No love here. A single neat bed. A wooden chair. Beneath the bed a pile of discarded books. Mine. No other furnishings.

The torchlight reveals Minnie sitting on the chair.

It was her room. And my heart was heavy. Bless you Peggy dear. Bless you.

MARGARET *suddenly appears. Stern. Terse. This is a side to her that is seldom shown.*

MARGARET. Mrs Christie. I fear Stringer has taken a turn for the worse. We will have to draw our evening to a close.

AGATHA. Is there anything I can do to help?

MARGARET. You've done enough.

Beat.

AGATHA. Something's upset you.

MARGARET. And you shouldn't be in here.

AGATHA. I know it has. Peggy?

MARGARET. This is a private room.

AGATHA. I apologise. I'd never intrude. Heaven forfend. But I thought you might need my assistance with dessert so I followed you and... got a trifle lost. It's such a delightful maze Nine Elms, isn't it? Part of its unique charm.

MARGARET. The words of his mouth were smoother than butter, but war was in his heart.

AGATHA. Sorry?

SPINSTER. *(aside to Agatha)* The psalms, dear. There's one for every occasion.

MARGARET. You have been deceiving me.

AGATHA. Me? Why would I?

    MARGARET *thrusts the paper at her.*

MARGARET. Today's *Times*. And page three! Tuft tried to hide it from me because he was disappointed. But not half as disappointed as I am.

    AGATHA *reads.*

AGATHA. Oh good heavens... I was asked to make an official statement.

MARGARET. The matter feels all the more troubling with the use of the word "official".

AGATHA. How stupid of me. I had no idea it was the press asking. You know what rascals they are. And my secretary can be a shade tardy when it comes to the essential details.

MARGARET. How wicked. First you lie. Then you blame others for your own failings.

AGATHA. Peggy!

MARGARET. "Mrs Christie thinks Margaret Rutherford is a fine actress but she bares no resemblance to Miss Marple as she imagines her". These are words I will never forget.

AGATHA. It was never meant to be printed... damned press. I expect more from The Times. Don't you?

MARGARET All that remains to be said is to bid each other good night.

AGATHA. No, Peggy. What about the blancmange? I tell you what... you can have Mrs Bunny's tail. No arguments.

MARGARET. And take these wretched things with you too.

    MARGARET *grabs the books. She thrusts them in* **AGATHA**'s *direction during the following.*

AGATHA. This may be a case of double standards.

MARGARET. I have done nothing to distress you.

AGATHA It is obviously acceptable for you to tell the press you think my work is sordid but when I....

MARGARET. Murder is sordid. Even one who relishes sullying their soul with it so rashly should agree with that.

AGATHA. Murder is my way of examining the human condition.

MARGARET Along with meddling into other people's private lives. Here you are prying and poking about behind my back, searching for who knows what.

AGATHA This is a dreadful misunderstanding.

MARGARET I need you to leave our home. Now.

AGATHA This anger proves you have something to hide.

MARGARET. We should never have met like this. We need to remember we are professionals. We operate in different worlds. They happen to be bisecting each other currently. But it's a fleeting thing.

AGATHA. I only want to help.

MARGARET. I'm sure you find magnanimous gestures deeply satisfying but Miss Margaret Rutherford doesn't need anyone's help.

AGATHA. I don't want our friendship to end. Not like this.

MARGARET. Of course you don't. It hasn't quite given you what you pursued it to attain. You haven't heard enough of my story...

AGATHA. No.

MARGARET. But what would you do once it was fully in your clutches?

AGATHA. That's not the reason.

MARGARET. Send a follow up comment to *The Times*?

AGATHA. I don't want it our friendship to end. Because ...Well, isn't it a lonely business?

MARGARET. We have work to do.

AGATHA. Being us?

    Pause.

MARGARET. You keep your Miss Marple to yourself. I'll do the same with mine.

SPINSTER. There's plenty of her to go around.

MARGARET *and* **AGATHA** Not now old woman..

Pause. There's a moment when the pair register they both heard the **SPINSTER**. *This almost brings them back together.*

MARGARET. I will call for your car. I'm sure you'll be able to find your own way out.

MARGARET *goes.* **AGATHA** *joins* **SPINSTER** *again.*

SPINSTER. All my efforts to bring you together. Dashed. But all is not lost.

AGATHA. It certainly feels that way. I fear she'll never speak to me again.

SPINSTER. I'm not talking about Peggy. I'm referring to you. You almost made quite a confession. You've needed someone who understands for some time.

AGATHA. No. I won't be beaten by this. I will unearth Miss Margaret Rutherford's secret.

SPINSTER. After all, that's conceivably the only way you'll ever face your own.

Pause.

AGATHA. I'm not letting this story go.

AGATHA *leaves.*

SPINSTER. Hang on to your britches as they say in the Penny Dreadfuls. The game is now, well and truly afoot.

Oh but I promised to tell you the rest of my tale... Our dear gentlemen... well, far be it for me to disappoint.

MARGARET *joins her.*

So the gentlemen failed to surface. The eggs and bacon spoiled. After several hours of mounting concern for her delightful guests Mrs Marchant, their landlady, sent her husband up to their room.

A door on the set rattles but remains closed. Someone is clearly behind it. **MARGARET** *and the* **SPINSTER** *approach it and we hear someone struggling to catch their breath.*

MARGARET. Someone behind the door was breathing heavily.

Sobbing. Shuffling. The son, my father

The sound of the breathing increases as music builds.
MARGARET *reaches out to open the door. As she touches the doorknob... Blackout.*

ACT TWO

Scene One

 MARGARET *appears.*

MARGARET. I will now present, by way of a diversion, Miss Margaret Rutherford's guide to successful marriage.

 First and foremost… marry a much younger man.

 AGATHA *appears.*

AGATHA. I married an archaeologist. The older I get the more interested in me he becomes.

MARGARET. Tuft is seven years my junior. Quite a catch I'm sure you'll agree.

 AGATHA *coughs* **MARGARET** *glares at her.*

AGATHA. Terribly dry up here isn't it? Go on. Continue…

MARGARET. He's the eternal boy.

AGATHA. Ah but men folk don't get cluttered up with things like we women do.

MARGARET. Make sure your husband is more than a husband.

AGATHA. An arrangement. You have to decide to compromise.

MARGARET. He should be a friend, an adequate cook, a brother… a dear little…

 Pause. **AGATHA** *notices this with interest.*

AGATHA. Learn how to turn a blind eye.

MARGARET. Do things together. Relish each other's companionship.

AGATHA. Choose someone who won't leave.

MARGARET. Go for long walks. Share a love of poetry, so good for the breathing and the soul. And although sharing is the lifeblood of marriage, be comfortable away from each other safe in the knowledge that your union is solid. I am fond of taking spells at a health spa. I go alone… It refreshes the spirit.

AGATHA. Protect each other. In the public eye, this is crucial.

MARGARET. I face cruelty on a daily basis. A journalist once wrote that if I were to be transformed into a gargoyle on Notre Dame I'd make the rest look like Audrey Hepburn. Seldom has a day passed when Tuft doesn't praise my glorious physicality. He admires my body. I know he's making me feel better. I also know I am beautiful in so many ways. Outside I'm Miss Margaret Rutherford. Inside I'm Jane Russell.

AGATHA. Don't be afraid to enjoy the company of other members of the opposite sex.

MARGARET. Or have your head turned by dashing strangers.

AGATHA. I wouldn't go that far.

MARGARET. I've danced with princes, been romanced by maestros. All harmless. More or less. Yearning for beauty is a natural compulsion.

AGATHA. If you can be bothered with that sort of thing.

MARGARET. Finally. Sleep alone. Always.

AGATHA. Absolutely.

MARGARET. Follow these few simple rules and a lifetime of bliss awaits...

AGATHA. It does?

MARGARET. It truly does.

The **SPINSTER** *appears.*

SPINSTER. Darning someone else's socks? Fathoming out balanced recipes for three square meals a day week in week out.? Ignoring the abundant passage of early hours gas under the quilt. Pretending to be interested in the mumblings of the male species. No. In my humble opinion I find the whole notion of marriage far less digestible than murder. Which is ironic as it so often leads to murder. Now that doesn't mean I haven't... Well... you know? Probably more gentleman callers than the two of them put together. Well there was a war on. I felt I had to play my part when it came to comforting our brave So to resume our tale my dears...

A pair of famous ladies have reluctantly met through the imagined force of a spirited spinster with a flair for the grisly.

Despite the anticipated pattern of events they become acquainted. Dare I say, friends? They spend time together. And Agatha, her brilliant mind firing on all cylinders, slowly inches closer to the truth. To Peggy's story. Which, as you've probably fathomed out for yourselves, involves murder most foul. A terrible crime committed within her own family.

Such a nuisance about their little falling out. I feel the urge to meddle once again. Well needs must. Otherwise we'll be here all night.

Scene Two

The music shifts. The exotic sounds we heard at the beginning. As lights come back up **MARGARET** *once again sleeps. An extravagant bouquet is on a table nearby. She wakes up with a jolt.*

MARGARET. Back again, Tuft... back in the shadow of the tamarind tree. The air is thick with heat. Humid. Not even a trickle of a breeze, every leaf is deathly still. I'm scared. To look up. Eyes shut. Then there's a knocking... suddenly I'm in Aunt Bessie's hall in Wimbledon about to answer the heavy oak front door. I'm happy. Really happy. At this moment I haven't a single care, not one... but as I reach out my trembling hand I have a creeping sense of dread...

Tuft? Tuft?

She spies Minnie. Picks her up.

It's Tuesday. Daddy has an appointment in town with Johnny Gielgud. Your Uncle Johnny? Remember? You have such a laugh with him. When he talks to you in his silly voice. Pretends to throw you across the room until I squeal. A terrible tease. Boys will be...

She rocks Minnie. Half sings a rhyme to her under her breath.

I wish Stringer were here. My scenes today are especially gruelling. I've told them... they think it's my way of being difficult because, as Pearl says, they expect actresses to behave like that. But I never would...

The violence is mounting Minnie. As I knew it would. As I feared. This has been my worry. What the dreadful happenings are stirring up. I can't ignore it.

Today I will find a woman of roughly my own age skewered to her favourite seat by a hat pin. You wouldn't believe the genteel lady who would tell me saucy jokes whilst polishing off my brandy snaps would be capable of such inventions...

The **SPINSTER** *has joined her with her knitting.*

SPINSTER. Oh you don't know the half dear.

MARGARET. I know more than I care to. She'll kill anything for a good story. I perused the reading material she left me. My dreams were worse than ever after that.

SPINSTER. You are in the wars aren't you?

MARGARET. I don't especially wish to talk to you.

SPINSTER. Well, like it or not you are. And about time too.

MARGARET. I can't tell anyone… I never will. It's impossible.

SPINSTER. Are you certain of that?

MARGARET. Not even Minnie. What's inside must stay. To explain it would feed it. It would become another way of losing….. losing everything.

Pause.

Only Tuft has come close. But he doesn't really understand. He says he does but it's clear in his eyes that he doesn't. Stringer and I. We have such a history he says. A history. It makes us strong. No one wants a past. They want a future. Even at my age.

Pause.

If only he'd hold me. Sometimes. Touch me….

Pause.

SPINSTER. You miss Agatha…

MARGARET. Minnie misses her. I can't say I do. Catching her like that prying. I was agitated in the extreme. I'm afraid I used some ireful terminology.

SPINSTER. It's what you needed.

MARGARET. There can be no turning back after such a scene.

SPINSTER Nonsense. Letting off a bit of steam. That's all.

Sudden knock on a door. The pair look at each other. The **SPINSTER** *ventures forth and after a beat screams. The scream turns into a cry of pleasure. She has discovered a bouquet of flowers and presents them to* **MARGARET**.

SPINSTER. Oh… such lovely flowers.

MARGARET. A sincere apology.

SPINSTER. And an invitation to take tea?

MARGARET. Claridges. Excellent scones and a sublime gooseberry conserve. Most acceptable. But she's getting too close.

SPINSTER. Would that be such a bad thing?

MARGARET. She's clever. She looks at me. Her looks... But perhaps... Perhaps?

SPINSTER. Good girl.

MARGARET. Aunt Bessie always knows best.

Scene Three

AGATHA *talks to the* SPINSTER.

AGATHA. I started this quest to serve my own ends. I feel some degree of shame about this. But when you write you're forever honing in on possibilities. Once the antennae tune in, you can't stop it. You steal fragments of people's lives and stitch them together. The friendship has become genuine. I hope she knows that. But still the scent of a story beckons me on. Peggy as a child, plus some undisclosed event had merged to equal Margaret Rutherford. This is the formula I need to crack. There's so much more to her than the warmly bundled bulldog adored by so many.

We're in Claridges. AGATHA *joins* MARGARET *at a table. The* SPINSTER *is with them knitting silently. We hear the clink and bustle of the hotel dining room.*

MARGARET. Of course Lilian Bayliss gave me Lady Capulet where I could do "least damage", as she said under her brandy breath. I still heard. I wasn't one of her favourites. Not one of the girls she took to her inner sanctum and prayed with. But I should have been Juliet. I understood her. I had the emotional capacity.

AGATHA. When was this?

MARGARET. 1926.

AGATHA. But you'd have been... thirty odd in 1926.

MARGARET. Beauty and innocence comes from within. My Juliet would have distracted the audience from the physical presence.
Beat.
And I didn't look much different when I was sixteen. When you're born with a face like mine you have to embrace it. Learn to live with it.

AGATHA. Take it on the wobbly chins...

MARGARET. Cheers to that.
They chink tea cups..

AGATHA. I've missed you.

MARGARET. This has been the most delicious tea. I insist on paying.

AGATHA. I insist on Agatha Christie paying. Agatha Christie Limited that is. I have discreet little expensive accounts all over town. Never questioned. The corporate buffoons wouldn't dare.

MARGARET. The gooseberry jam! I wonder if they sell it.

AGATHA. . I hardly think Claridges would do anything so parochial.

MARGARET. Of course not. Such a pity.

Pause.

AGATHA. There's plenty left in the pot. Slip it in your bag. Go on.

MARGARET. Agatha! I couldn't...

AGATHA. Oh go on. I won't tell.

MARGARET. It would spill. I've so much in here that might spoil.

AGATHA. Wrap it tightly in a napkin.

MARGARET. And steal that too?

AGATHA. Go on. They won't care. And they won't suspect pensioners of pilfering. Not a couple as dignified and as famous as us.

AGATHA *places a napkin over the jam pot.* MARGARET *pretends to sneeze and nicks the pot, thrusting it into her bag. She and* AGATHA *giggle like girls.*

It's nice to see you so happy.

MARGARET. I'm always happy. Why wouldn't I be happy? As long as there's a sea to swim in, a poetry book to devour... I've had a wonderful life... having. I've told you about delightful Elizabeth Taylor and delicious Mr Richard Burton...?

AGATHA. Darling.

MARGARET. Agatha... please...

AGATHA. When I said I wanted to help.

MARGARET. Please... I implore you...

AGATHA. It's because I understand.

Pause.

MARGARET. I need no help. I'm fully in control of my fate.

AGATHA. You know I have secrets too. One that remains a mystery today. I've never told anyone. Not the truth. But many years ago. The same year you were so desperate to play Juliet... well...

MARGARET. Edith Evans was in the same company. She thought I could do it. She said as much.

AGATHA. I disappeared. Vanished. Quite completely.

MARGARET. Of course you had to watch Evans. A propensity for the stealing of scenes. And roles. Got to Cleopatra before me. Not one of her best.

AGATHA. They said I'd done it to help the book sales. Rot. I never needed any help in that department.

MARGARET. In fact they could have called Edith Evans performance as Cleopatra, Death on the Nile. Forgive me. I'm being wicked.

AGATHA. Eleven days. Without a trace. Nobody's ever known where I went.

MARGARET. You don't need to tell me about it.

AGATHA. It became a matter of national concern. It was discussed in Parliament. The government enlisted other famous crime writers to help. Dotty Sayers actually used the story of my disappearance as the inspiration for one of her novels. I don't begrudge her that. So few original ideas of her own, she had it with my blessing. I wrote to her and told her this. She didn't write back.

Of the thirty six ways of avoiding disaster running away *isn't* the best.

SPINSTER. If you want to hear Margaret's truth you need to face your own. Tell her Agatha. Tell her. Tell her now

AGATHA *changes her mind about revealing her secret.*

AGATHA. I was undercover. Joined the circus as a lady lion tamer. No one suspected that under the Big Top hid a highly organised band of Bolsheviks headed by a forty-two-stone bearded lady.

MARGARET. You are very droll Agatha dear. But look at the time. It passes so very swiftly when we're together. I need to head home.

AGATHA. Don't you want to hear the rest?

MARGARET. Stringer will be preparing supper shortly. Can't manage the tin opener. Doesn't have the wrist action.

AGATHA. I know about secrets. How they can be a terrible thing.

SPINSTER. You're incorrigible Agatha.

MARGARET. I suppose to create such a lurid fantasy the real secret must be quite dreadful.

SPINSTER. Not as daft as she pretends is she?

MARGARET. Some things are best buried. Hidden. Some things can't and shouldn't be spoken of. Perhaps it's the only way to make sure they won't happen again.

MARGARET *goes.*

Scene Four

AGATHA. That could have gone better.

SPINSTER. You've only got yourself to blame.

AGATHA. Get on with your knitting old woman.

SPINSTER. I've never been one to mince my words. If you can't be honest with yourself then you can't expect others...

AGATHA. As it happens I am slowly putting the pieces together without Margaret's help. I have been taking mental notes carefully during our meetings. I've also discovered certain facts by adding up fractions of information. The health spa she told me she was so fond of frequenting...

MARGARET. I always emerge refreshed and ready to take on the world. I swear it's what has given my career such longevity.

AGATHA. A sanatorium. Depression. Electro therapy. There's something she wants so desperately to burn from her memory she's willing to fry her brain.

And she not only collect's things... people too. A set of very suspect hangers-on chosen with myopic abandonment. Gordon Langley Simmons. A minor novelist with a knack for preying on wealthy dowagers. A self-proclaimed hermaphrodite.

MARGARET. Very expensive business.

AGATHA. To which you no doubt contributed.

MARGARET. She's a medical anomaly.

AGATHA. There was a pianist.

MARGARET. A maestro. A genius.

AGATHA. Peggy was besotted with him. Another foolish affair of the heart.

MARGARET. He led me on in Denmark. Not very gentlemanly.

AGATHA. A collection of rough and ready borstal boys.

MARGARET. Stringer's choice.

AGATHA. And then there was an unusual brush with royalty.

Scene Five

Romantic waltz music.

SPINSTER. The story of Miss Margaret Rutherford and the Prince.
MARGARET. A beguiling romance.

His gracious highness Prince Juan, bronzed, blonde and beautiful, practically waltzed into my life at a time when, I must say, I was in need of a smattering of blue-eyed wonderment. The younger brother of King Hussein of Jordan, regrettably estranged, swept into my dressing room with a flourish, and so started a magnificent magic carpet ride to lands and experiences I could never have even imagined. He entertained us with tales of his youth, glorious temples and opulent palaces. And I'd dance with him when the opportunity arose.

He'd often join us for our three am suppers. I often wondered how a Muslim could so heartily tuck into bacon. But I daresay he'd sacrifice his most fundamental beliefs to be polite. The champagne made one pause for thought too. He could get through gallons. But in certain situations it would be vulgar not to.

He lavished us with gifts by way of thanks for our generosity. He took delight in silver trinkets and also gave us dear Nicodemus. He so very much wanted to be a part of our lives and he believed that through the cat we could feel he was there wherever our travels took us.

Dancing...

I remember our dancing best of all. His lovely arms held me and there was always magic in the air. Then midnight struck.

We called the Jordanian Embassy. We were told quite bluntly, there was no Prince Juan.

Music ends abruptly.

He hadn't even left a slipper on the stair.

Scene Six

AGATHA. Silver Al, as they called her "Prince" on the black market. An antiques dealer from the sleazier side of the Portobello Road. He'd served time for fraud.

She mostly shrugged bad behaviour off with a tiny laugh. She did it with the entire gallery of wastrels and miscreants who shadowed her and Stringer's lives. They fitted in with their eccentricities seamlessly, siphoning off what they could along the way. She couldn't or wouldn't acknowledge bad in anyone. But when we discussed the tales of her unhealthy acolytes, I'd detect the disappointment cross her face like a whisper. I would.

However alarming these stories were, they weren't the roots of the problem. They existed because of these roots. Poisoned buds that would never bloom into anything... wholesome.

When I finally started to unearth the truth it came about by chance.

I'd been invited to a soirée. That's how they described it on the invitation. Soirée. A publisher's bash. My limiters insisted I attend. There were a few bridges to be built. But a whole glut of publishers in one room. What would be the collective noun for that? A defecation perhaps? Although I've been known to use that already. For agents.

We're at a publisher's soirée. Music in the background. The muted sound of conversation. **AGATHA** *clearly doesn't want to be there. She's with a well-coiffed woman... the* **SPINSTER** *in disguise again.* **AGATHA** *is trying to ignore her. Someone sees her from across the room. She offers a smile and a little wave.*

SPINSTER. So as I was saying I've been a huge, huge fan.

AGATHA. How sweet.

SPINSTER. Of course only since *Murder She Said* came out. Oh Margaret Rutherford makes me laugh and laugh. When she pulls those faces as Miss Marple.

AGATHA. Do you always wear your hair like that?

SPINSTER. Yes I do. And the shade. Autumn conker. Goes with my nail polish look.

AGATHA. Good to have a few details because I'm going to write about you one day.

SPINSTER. Ooo-oo. Mr Wedgwood-Benn!... Having a nice time?

She's distracted waving to her boss so doesn't hear AGATHA *say the following.*

AGATHA. I'm going to kill you. Cyanide. Sparkling of course. Won't waste anything original.

SPINSTER. That's my boss Mr Wedgwood-Benn. He's been through it. What with his son Tony. You know. Being a leftie. Kiddie's books. That's what we specialise in. E Nesbit. *The Railway Children. Phoenix and the Carpet.* Read them all to my little ones. Such a clever chap and still ever such a good seller.

AGATHA. E. Nesbit is a woman.

SPINSTER. He can't be.

AGATHA. And it will be a cold day in hell before a saccharine swilled tale for tots outsells my efforts.

SPINSTER. Of course Miss Rutherford's related to the Wedgwood-Benn's. You know that don't you? And you probably know about the problems. Her poor Dad. But I shouldn't gossip.

AGATHA. Have another glass of fizz.

SPINSTER. It's going to my head already. But if you insist and I might as well make the most of it. I'm only in the typing pool. We drew straws to see who got to come here and I won.

AGATHA. So. Miss Rutherford's poor Dad.

SPINSTER. William Wedgwood-Benn. That was his name originally. But he had to change it afterwards. Well you would have to wouldn't you. Such a shocking business. So he became Mr Rutherford.

It was all rather gruesome. You know. What he did.

AGATHA. Tell me?

SPINSTER. Like something out of one of your books. He got committed. Then he moved to India when he was released. He and his young wife went there together. That's where Margaret Rutherford was born...

AGATHA *moves away from the* SPINSTER.

AGATHA. It was time for me to leave.

I began investigating the Wedgwood-Benn's the very next day... I have excellent resources at my disposal and a tenacious research technique. It wasn't too long before I discovered some scant newspaper accounts and I was able to piece together details of a terrible tragedy.

Music builds. **SPINSTER** *moves centre still in the guise of the woman at the party.*

SPINSTER. It was the son, in the bedroom with the chamber pot...

AGATHA. An innocent household item used for deadly intent.

He'd brought it down on the Reverend's head. Again and again and again.

SPINSTER. Again and again and again.

Music builds as **SPINSTER** *vigorously mimes the murder.*

Scene Seven

MARGARET *and* **AGATHA** *are alone. This time they're on the set. Filming has finished for the day.* **MARGARET** *has made tea on a primus stove and they're on deckchairs. They're silent for a while.*

MARGARET. I like this. When we sit and say nothing.

Pause.

What're you thinking?

AGATHA. Only how I've made murder my business. Over forty years.

MARGARET. I act because I couldn't live without it. It must be the same for you.

AGATHA. But my experience of murder has always been second hand. I'm blessed. Whatever my imagination may stir up, will never be as bad as the reality of violence.

Pause.

Tell me about your family? And not the stuffed menagerie, dear.

Pause.

You don't seem surprised by my question?

MARGARET. I was expecting it. Maybe even hoping you'd ask it.

AGATHA. Start by telling me about India.

Pause. **MARGARET** *works out how before she begins.*

MARGARET. We were so happy. My father. My mother Florence, as fragile as a lily… me, and there would have been…

She'd wanted a boy. Near where we lived was a ruined temple in a tea garden long since deserted because of a curse. Here there lived a fakir who was skilled in the dark arts and mother knew only he could help. She went at night. He gave her a snake bone for under her pillow. He told her, her wish would come true. She believed him. So I did too.

Our garden. I still dream of it. At the bottom stood a wise tamarind tree stretching across the length of a deep red wall. But I was so very young when they both died.

More tea?

AGATHA *takes her hand.*

AGATHA. Go further back Peggy. What happened to your father? Why did he kill your grandfather?

MARGARET. I can't...

Pause. AGATHA *decides to share her secret.*

AGATHA. My Archie. The boy with the dimple in his chin. That's one of the things I fell immediately in love with. First sight isn't an invention of the romantics. It happened to me. I still hear his voice. Only its cold. And it doesn't say what I want to hear.

"I love her. Not you. Not anymore. I want a divorce"... How had I failed? I'd devoted myself to him. What was mine was his and my success... my love for him fuelled my success. But it drove him away. He chose her. Not me. Not the daughter I'd given him. Her. She'd never overshadow him.

This is hard for me. Archie passed very recently... You see I'd never given up hope of... not entirely. And when his other woman died before him I had to stop myself feeling such joy. Hope... And up until that point and since, I've always believed one should live ones life trying not to do anybody any harm along the way.

I did run away. When I vanished there wasn't any mystery. None at all. I knew what I was doing and I fled because I was dying inside. If I stayed one night longer... It wasn't safe. Not for me. My little girl. Not for him. My one love. I saw into the mind of someone who could commit an act of evil. It was my mind. I had no choice.

But even after I left. I worked it all out you see. How to kill Archie without ever being found guilty

MARGARET. Where did you go?

AGATHA. There were days I can't remember. Pain so terrible. But when I emerged from the fog and I knew he was under suspicion for my murder I kept on going. In my mind he deserved to be hanged for what he'd done. So I let the case against him build whilst I enjoyed such freedom... I came so close to seeing it through to the end.

MARGARET. But you stopped yourself?

AGATHA. I was found.

Pause.

Archibald drove all the way to Harrogate to collect me. He was a broken man. I took the train back home. Alone.

So I understand. Know that some troubles become buried in order for one to... survive.

But they shouldn't stay there. There needs to be peace.

Pause.

Reverend Julius Benn was murdered by his son William. Your father. The killing had been brutal. It was deemed an act of insanity. William who had been troubled with mental illness was committed to Broadmoor. His wife would wait for him.

MARGARET. The press can never find out. It will destroy my career.

AGATHA. No wonder you wanted to avoid any connection to murder. This event must still haunt you terribly.

MARGARET. How could it? It happened before I even existed.

Pause. AGATHA's *taken aback.*

AGATHA. Well yes... but surely...

MARGARET. No, no my dear Agatha, You don't understand. How could something that took place so long before I was born affect me so profoundly?

My torment doesn't lie in the murder but the ripples it caused to flow through my life. It's what happened next that has haunted me.

The following begins with the ballad underscored and delivered in the style adopted by Rutherford during a sequence in Murder Most Foul. *Slowly she drops the bravado and her true devastation starts to show.*

SPINSTER. The creation of Miss Margaret Rutherford. A dramatic ballad.

MARGARET.

Born to parents whom she gave fresh hope to,
Who'd fled to a strange foreign clime,
Our girl Peg's life was quite wondrous
'Til shadows fell bringing the terrible time.

Her father's past was where it belonged,
Tho' he'd always regret his dread crime,
For now he was cured, had a future at last

'Til madness brought back the terrible time.

While living in joy in a mystical land
The blessing of a new child did chime
But the mother sought solace in the tamarind tree
Her body swayed to the tune of the terrible time.

From then Peggy's world did unravel
Her father lost all reason and rhyme
Transported back home in a blanket of woe
Awaiting the dawn of her own...

MARGARET *stops. She's emotional. She sits down again. Recovers.*

MARGARET. Poetry. So good for the breathing. And the soul.

My life has been one of illustrious diversion. That's, in all probability why Miss Margaret Rutherford exists... To divert...

The murder committed by my father was a terrible thing. But not evil. I truly believe...

AGATHA. He was incredibly ill.

MARGARET. And he was given a second chance. It was claimed he was cured. They began a new life, he and my mother. A happy one. I know it was. And it should have continued...

My mother took her own life also killing her unborn baby.

AGATHA. Oh Peggy...

MARGARET. Walked out of the house into the garden and hanged herself at sunset. No warning. No explanation. After this my father's illness returned with a vengeance.

AGATHA. What happened?

MARGARET. Managed the passage home with me, a precious parcel he kept under his arm all the way... somehow. He left me with Aunt Bessie before he.... I don't know how he did it. How he got us both back intact..

AGATHA. He must have loved you. So much...

MARGARET. I was thirteen. An orphan. This much I knew. But a happy child. Very happy until that Sunday afternoon...

AGATHA. Tell me....

MARGARET. I was thirteen. Almost an adult. Bessie was in the kitchen. I knew I wasn't meant to open the door under any circumstances. But what would be the harm in it? Just this once. As I went down the hallway music played in the parlour....I sang along. Me and Bessie's current favourite song.

She half sings.

"Who Stole My Heart Away, Who makes me dream all day..."

There was a stranger. In rags. Skin and bones. Yellowed teeth. Dishevelled but not unkind "I'm here for your father Peggy," he said. "He loves you."

I replied most emphatically. He's dead. But I think I understood. In an instant. The elephant stampede. Malaria. Native uprising. Suddenly all the reasons that had been offered to my innocent ears to explain my orphaned state jangled in my head.

"Billy Rutherford aint dead. He's in Broadmoor."

Aunt Bess, tight lipped when I told her I'd answered the door to a stranger, decided I needed the truth. Every scrap. She told me with a manner that can only be described as forensic. She was a simple soul. She didn't know how else to handle this unfortunate happening. I sat in silence and listened. Took it all like the adult I'd so quickly become. I shed one tear when I heard about the baby. No more. I had questions but couldn't find a way of asking them. I doubt they'd have been answered.

AGATHA. All these years. My dear friend.

MARGARET. The murder. That's been a worry. That threatened Margaret Rutherford most. Salacious stories have so much appeal.

But Peggy. Who I really am. No one has ever known how I feel. Really feel... How frightened I became from that moment on...

She picks up Minnie and cradles her. Hums Who? *by Jerome Kern to her. Pause.*

AGATHA. What became of your father?

MARGARET. I was never allowed to see him. Even when I knew the truth... I think that hurts most of all. I could have seen first-hand that however terrible the world is around you, you can survive. It's within you. I struggle to forgive Aunt Bess for that. If only I'd been able to see him again. Once. That would have been enough...

My fears have always been about madness. Not violence. My father and my mother both had terrible deadly aberrations... What if the same fate awaited me...

AGATHA. I'm certain...

MARGARET. It's in me. It has to be. I need to avoid situations where my thoughts will take me back... I have to prevent the insanity from breaking through... At all costs.

I'd have loved a baby boy. My brother. We'd have been friends. I know we would. We'd have shared everything.

More half whispered lullaby. **AGATHA** *holds her friend.*

I've been blessed. I've had a glorious life as Miss Margaret Rutherford.

Glorious.

The lights go half down on **MARGARET** *and* **AGATHA.**

Scene Eight

MARGARET *and* **AGATHA** *remain centre in half light.*

SPINSTER. It's getting late. I promised my doctor I wouldn't strain my eyes and I'd cut back on the old...

She holds up the empty decanter.

Oh shame on me.

I intend to respect most of this young doctor's wishes. Partly for the sake of self-discipline, because where would we be without that. But also I rather like the boy. He's got what I call staying power. One of the very few doctors, where I'm from, who hasn't been done in or hanged for... well you know.

Lights up... The three ladies start to clear the set into the state we first found it.

MARGARET. She finally got her way.

AGATHA. Always do.

MARGARET. Can't say I blame her. *Murder Ahoy* was the fourth and last Miss Marple feature.

AGATHA. A farrago of nonsense. Things went from bad to worse at a staggering rate of knots. Tolerated the first picture. Wouldn't see the second. Based on *After the Funeral* they told me. There was a funeral. And it was at the start... that's the only resemblance to my original plot. And they set it in a riding school. I said to Pollock... "Don't kill Rutherford off with too many outdoor sports will you?" He laughed. Very, very nervously.

MARGARET. Initially they had humoured my efforts to crank up the tension, because they felt sure the laughter wouldn't be far behind. And they were correct. From the moment in the second picture when Tuft and I did that blasted twist, the crew laughed so loud I knew I was fighting a losing battle.

AGATHA. When I publish *At Bertram's Hotel* I'll give it a pointed subtitle "Featuring Miss Marple, the original character as created by Agatha Christie. I do, after all, have a little experience with plots, dialogue, and knowing what audiences like, you know." The oafs at MGM trampled my spinster into the ground. Not Peggy.

SPINSTER. Go on say it dear. You know you want to.

AGATHA. Well... she was rather good. She really was.

MARGARET. And having Miss Marple in my life? This adventure's made my name bigger than I ever imagined possible... the offers of work... well they've overwhelmed me. Mr Orson Welles... the great Chaplin. Hollywood... I was frightfully good in *The VIP's*, but it was little more than a cameo. I couldn't believe it when I actually won... let me find it... where is he? My golden boy.

AGATHA. You were using it as a doorstop.

MARGARET *produces an Oscar from somewhere.*

MARGARET. Hello Oscar! "Hello Peggy my love."

This will end up being stolen the year after I die.

AGATHA. Her blinkered approach to those she became close to will carry on beyond the grave.

MARGARET. After I pass, Tuft will be cajoled into marrying Violet our sixty-five-year-old housekeeper. He'll die before this can happen, she'll forge the will, flog a heap of valuables, jump bail and be a wanted felon for the rest of her days. The truth.

AGATHA. Even I could make that up.

MARGARET. I will die having lost my mind. It won't be easy to begin with. Like lowering yourself into a hot bath. But once I get so far... Minnie and I will sit in the sun. A breeze upon my face. My favourite poems jumbled up. A sense of contentment. Of realising I had been loved. Of so much forgotten never to be recalled.

AGATHA. After Margaret forgets herself I'll keep in touch by writing to Stringer asking him to read her my letters.

AGATHA. Eventually I'll lose the plot too. Cast away my genteel English Lady ways. Cut off my hair, be honest to the point of embarrassment and frequently try to solve the case of Lord Lucan.

MARGARET. Tuft's last wish will be to be buried with the sealed letter he's always carried around with him in the top pocket of his jacket. From ruddy Johnny Gielgud. Tuft's wish, unfortunately, will not be carried out.

I replaced the precious letter with one from me years ago. And it's far more colourful than Johnny's effort!

AGATHA. And as for my characters. My creations...

SPINSTER. The demise of the Belgian will finally become public

AGATHA. I kept nipping back to the vault at Coutts and changing the end. Finally I gave him a graceful send off. When everything's said and done he'd been good to me.

SPINSTER. Miss Marple will end up in the same vault as Poirot. But she'll survive her last adventure. She'll be going strong for many decades to come.

AGATHA. Like me, Margaret will die a Dame.

MARGARET. My gong will be granted first.

Pause.

AGATHA. I never saw my friend again.

MARGARET. Though I'd so often think of her.

SPINSTER. So our tale has reached its conclusion. Bitter sweet unfortunately. But if there's one thing my isolated life on the side lines has taught me; there's no such thing as a truly happy ending. At best you may find one you're able to live with.

AGATHA. Oh and I did get a story. After our meeting I kept thinking… movie stars. Such fragile creatures… Well I couldn't help myself. I decided to think of it as a gift. One to honour our marvellous friendship

She hands **MARGARET** *a book.*

MARGARET. *The Mirror Crack'd From Side to Side* by Agatha Christie.

SPINSTER. Hemlock. In the cocktails.

AGATHA. That's the one. Look inside. Go on.

MARGARET *does and reads the inscription.*

MARGARET. For Margaret Rutherford. In admiration. How touching. It'll be a staggering work I'm sure.

Miss Marple at her very best…

How thrilling… though of course, I'll never read it.

Music builds

AGATHA *and* **MARGARET** *laugh as the lights slowly fade.*

The End

PROPERTY PLOT

ACT 1

Debris and forgotten old furniture
Old set saved from a scrap heap
Comfy chair
Cosy lighting
Old upright piano with cover
Cover to cover chair, lighting, piano
Knitting
Key that doesn't work
Phone
Typewriter
Cape
Scarf
Very full glass of sherry
Tea
Tea cups x2
Saucer x2
Milk and milk jug
Teaspoon
Sugar and sugar bowl
Tea trolley
Tiny black book
Cake containing walnuts
Cake slice
Plates x2
Dessert forks x2
Books x6
Walnut without shell
Stuffed toy bunny
Pull cord behind a screen
Army of stuffed toys
The Times newspaper

ACT 2

Filled decanter
Extravagant bouquet on the table
Table as in Claridges
Jam pot
Tea on Stove
Deckchairs
Empty decanter
Oscar award
Sealed letter
Book

SOUND EFFECTS PLOT

ACT 1

Miss Marple theme tune recording
Faint evocative music (exotic sounds)
Christmas Bells ring out
Sound of pony and trap
Theme music
Theme music plays again
The clock chimes

ACT 2

Music shifts
Exotic sounds from the beginniing heard again
Clink and bustle of hotel dining room
Romantic waltz music
Music ends abruptly
Music in the background
Music builds

LIGHTING PLOT

ACT 1

Lights go down
Lights go up
Lights change
Lights down

ACT 2

Lights up
Lights go half down
Half light on Margaret and Agatha
Lights slowly fade

THIS IS NOT THE END

Visit samuelfrench.co.uk and discover the best theatre bookshop on the internet

A vast range of plays
Acting and theatre books
Gifts

samuelfrench.co.uk

samuelfrenchltd

samuel french uk

www.ingramcontent.com/pod-product-compliance
Ingram Content Group UK Ltd.
Pitfield, Milton Keynes, MK11 3LW, UK
UKHW021515020725
460240UK00008B/5